The Elephant's Ball

Illustrated by
Pauline Baynes

Eerdmans Books for Young Readers

Grand Rapids, Michigan • Cambridge, U. K.

For Charlotte

Illustrations © 2007 Pauline Baynes
Published in 2007 by Eerdmans Books for Young Readers,
an imprint of Wm. B. Eerdmans Publishing Co.

Wm. B. Eerdmans Publishing Co.
2140 Oak Industrial Dr. N.E., Grand Rapids, Michigan 49505
P.O. Box 163, Cambridge CB3 9PU U.K.

www.eerdmans.com/youngreaders

Manufactured in China

07 08 09 10 11   8 7 6 5 4 3 2 1

Library of Congress Cataloging-in-Publication Data

The elephant's ball / illustrated by Pauline Baynes.
p. cm.
Summary: A rhyming story about a grand party in the forest, given by the elephant and attended by all the animals.

ISBN: 978-0-8028-5316-5 (alk. paper)

[1. Balls (Parties) — Fiction. 2. Animals — Fiction. 3. Stories in rhyme.] I. Baynes, Pauline, ill..
PZ8.3.E383 2007
[E]--dc22
2006013767

Text type set in Bauer Bodini
Illustrations created with gouache

Gayle Brown, Art Director
Matthew Van Zomeren, Graphic Designer

Introduction

The Elephant's Ball was originally published in Great Britain in 1807 by John Harris, successor to the renowned publisher and bookseller John Newbery. This story-in-verse was part of a popular series of animal adventures which included other titles such as *The Butterfly's Ball* and *The Lion's Masquerade*. The books in this series, written simply to delight young readers, were innovative and became very popular.

The author of *The Elephant's Ball* is unknown — only the initials W. B. appear on the manuscript — but his or her original words are retained in this edition. Coupled with lively pictures from Pauline Baynes, the rhythm and charm of the nineteenth-century language comes to life. A glossary is included on the last page to help with unfamiliar terms.

The insects and birds, with the balls and their feasts
Caus'd much conversation among all the beasts.

The Elephant, famous for sense as for size,

At such entertainments express'd much surprise.

Says he, "Shall these impudent tribes of the air,

To break our soft slumbers thus wantonly dare?

Shall these petty creatures, us beasts far below,

Exceed us in consequence, fashion, and show?

Forbid it, true dignity, honor and pride!

A grand rural fête I will shortly provide,

That for pomp, taste, and splendor, shall far leave behind,

All former attempts at a similar kind."

The Buffalo, Bison, Elk, Antelope, Pard,

All heard what he spoke, with due marks of regard.

A number of messengers quickly he sent

To the beasts, far and near, to make known his intent.

The place he design'd for the scene of his plan

Was a valley remote from the dwellings of man:

Well guarded with mountains, embellish'd with trees,

And furnish'd with rivers that flow'd to the seas.

Here first came the Lion, so gallant and strong,

Well known by his mane that is shaggy and long;

The Jackall, his slave, follow'd close in his rear,

Resolv'd the good things with his master to share.

The Leopard came next — a gay sight to the eye,

With his coat spotted over like stars in the sky.

The Tiger his system of slaughter declin'd,

At once, a good supper and pleasure to find.

The bulky Rhinoceros came with his bride;

Well-armed with his horn, and his coat of mail hide.

Then came the Hyena, whose cries authors say

Oft lead the fond traveler out of his way,

Whom quickly he seizes and renders his prey.

The Wolf hasten'd hither, that Ruffian so bold,

Who kills the poor sheep when they stray from the fold.

The Bear having slept the long winter away,

Arriv'd from the north to be merry and gay.

The Panther ferocious, the Lynx of quick sight,

The Preacher and Glutton came hither that night.

The Camel, so often with burdens oppressed,

Was glad for a while from his labor to rest.

The Sloth, when invited, got up with much pain,

Just groan'd out, "Ah, No!" and then laid down again.

The Fox, near the hen-roost, no longer kept watch,

But hied to the feast, better viands to catch.

The Monkey, so cunning, and full of his sport,

To show all his talents came to this resort.

The Dog and Grimalkin from service releas'd,
Expected good snacks at the end of the feast.
The first at the gate, as a sentinel stood,
The last kept the Rats and the Mice from the food.
The crowd of strange quadrupeds seen at the ball,
'Twere tedious and needless to mention them all.
To shorten the story, suffice it to say
Some scores, nay some hundreds, attended that day.
But most of the tame and domestical kind
For fear of some stratagem, tarried behind.
Due caution is prudent! but laws had been made:
No Beast, on that night, should another invade.
Before we go further, 'tis proper to state
Each female was asked to attend with her mate.
Of these, many came to this fête of renown,
But some were prevented by causes well known.

Now Sol had retir'd to the ocean to sleep.

The Guests had arriv'd their gay vigils to keep.

Their hall was a lawn of sufficient extent,

Well skirted with trees, the rude winds to prevent.

The thick-woven branches deep curtains display'd,

And heaven's high arch a grand canopy made.

Some thousands of lamps, fix'd to poplars were seen,

That shone most resplendent red, yellow, and green.

When forms, introductions, and such were gone through,

'Twas quickly resolv'd the gay dance to pursue.

The musical band, on a terrace appearing,

Perform'd many tunes that enchanted the hearing.

The Ape on the haut-boy much science display'd,

The Monkey the fiddle delightfully play'd,

The Orang-Outang touch'd the harp with great skill,

The Ass beat the drum, with effect and good will,

And the Squirrel kept ringing his merry bells still.

The Elephant, stately, majestic, and tall,
With Cousin Rhinoceros open'd the ball.
With dignified mien the two partners advanc'd,
And the *De la Cour* minuet gracefully danc'd.
The Lion and Unicorn, beasts of great fame,
With much admiration accomplish'd the same.

The Tiger and Leopard, an active young pair,
Perform'd a brisk jig with an excellent air.

The Fox, Wolf, and Panther, their humors to please,
Danced three-hand'd reels with much spirit and ease.

Next Bruin stood up with a good natur'd smile,
And caper'd a horn-pipe in singular style,
With a staff in his paws, and erect all the while.

A few tried cotillions and such like French fancies,

But most of them join'd in John Bull's country dances.

Some beasts were not used to these violent motions,
And some were too old or too grave in their notions.
Of these a great many diverted their hours
With whist, lue, backgammon, quadrille, or all-fours.
Much time being spent in these pleasing diversions,
A motion was made to remit their exertions,
For supper was waiting; which, on this occasion,
Was manag'd with skill, and exact regulation.

The bosom of earth a firm table supply'd —

The cloth was green grass, with gay flow'rets bedy'd.

The various utensils by nature were cast,

And suited completely this antique repast.

The generous host had provided great plenty,

To suit various palates, of every dainty.

Some scores of fat oxen were roasted entire,

For those whose keen stomachs plain beef might require.

Profusion of veal, nice lamb, and good mutton,

To tickle the taste of each more refin'd glutton.

Abundance of fish, game, and poultry for those

Whose epicure palates such niceties chose.

Ripe fruits and rich sweet meats were serv'd in great store,

Of which much remain'd when the banquet was o'er.

For, as to mild foods of the vegetive kind,

Few guests at the table to these were inclin'd.

Rare hap for such persons as travell'd that way,

By chance or design, on the following day.

On wine and strong spirits few chose to regale,

As most were accustom'd to Adam's old ale.

When supper was ended, and each happy guest

Had freely partaken of what he lov'd best,

Of toasts and of sentiments various were giv'n:

As "Health to our Host, and the Land that we live in."

The former was drank with huzzas, three-times-three,

Which echo repeated with rapturous glee.

Now mirth and good humor pervaded the throng,

And each was requested to furnish a song,

Which many comply'd with; but such as deny'd,

Some whimsical laughable story supply'd.

The Lion, "Britannia Rule" sung mighty well;

The Tiger, "In English Roast Beef" did excel.

While others made all the wide valley to ring,

With "Nile's Glorious Battle" and "God Save the King."

In such good amusements the evening they past,

Till Aurora appear'd to the eastward at last;

When back to their homes, they return'd one and all,

Well pleas'd with the sports at the Elephant's Ball.

Glossary

Terms listed in the order they appear in the story

Pard: Leopard

Jackall: Coyote

Preacher and Glutton: slang terms for wild beasts

Viands: meats

Grimalkin: Cat

Sol: the Sun

Haut-boy: oboe

Ass: Donkey

De la Cour: French, literally meaning "of the heart," name of a piece of music

Bruin: Bear

Cotillions: type of dance for four couples in square formation, popular in the late 1700s

Whist, Lue, Backgammon, Quadrille, All-Fours: games popular during the seventeenth century

"Brittania Rule"; "In English Roast Beef"; "Nile's Glorious Battle": British songs popular in the 1700s

"God Save the King": (also called "God Save the Queen") Great Britain's national anthem

Aurora: the Morning